Freedom at Last!

How to Overcome
What's Holding You Back
From Getting What You Want

Freedom at Last!

How to Overcome What's Holding You Back From Getting What You Want

John Saye Smith Jr., RN, BSN

www.YouSpeakItPublishing.com

This material has been written and published solely for educational purposes. The author and the publisher shall have neither liability nor responsibility to any person or entity with respect to any loss, damage, or injury caused or alleged to be caused directly or indirectly by the information contained in this book.

The author of this book does not dispense medical advice or prescribe the use of any technique as a form of treatment for physical, emotional, or medical problems without the advice of a physician, either directly or indirectly. The intent of the author is only to offer information of a general nature to help the reader in the quest for well-being. In the event the reader uses any of the information in this book for self or others, which is a constitutional right, the author and the publisher assume no responsibility for the actions of the reader.

Statements made in this book have not been evaluated by the Food and Drug Administration. This book and its contents are not intended to diagnose, treat, or cure any infection, injury, or illness, or prevent any disease. Results vary and each person's experience is unique.

Statements made and opinions expressed in this publication are those of the author and do not necessarily reflect the views of the publisher or indicate an endorsement by the publisher.

ISBN: 978-1-945446-35-1

Praise for *Freedom at Last!*

"Life's true meaning comes from what you give rather than what you get. John's story beautifully illustrates for us how to get more meaning in our own lives while helping to enhance the lives of others. Reading this book will be time well spent."

— Betsy Westhafer, Publisher, ThoughtMasters Magazine, High Performance Coach, Marketing Executive at Savavo

"*Freedom at Last!* is truly a book for entrepreneurs who want to make an impact in their community."

— David Corbin, Keynote Speaker, Mentor to Mentors, Bestselling Author, Visionary, Inventor, Entrepreneur

"This book tells the story of one man's journey of self-discovery and is a 'must read' for those who are on their own path to finding true purpose in life."

— Justin Recla, Co-Founder, The Clear Business Directory, COO, The Recla Group, LLC

"John's story in *Freedom at Last!* from being a helpless immigrant to a successful entrepreneur is very compelling."

— Tina Brinkley Potts, Bestselling Author and Growth Strategist

"This book will show you how you can leverage empowerment and freedom."

— Dr. Charlie Webb, Leading Expert in Optimizing Health

"*Freedom at Last!* reminds me of the launch of the record-breaking *Rich Dad, Poor Dad*. We helped break those records. What is your LEGACY in life? You'll know when you read John's bestseller as a MUST have in your library. Buy five and give them to your best customers as you become UNFORGETTABLE by sharing this book."

— Berny Dohrmann, Founder, Forbes & Inc Magazine's #1 Ranked, CEO Space International

In this book, John decodes the concept of what freedom truly means!

— Lin Van Gelder, Retired Professional

"*Freedom at Last!* helps you reposition yourself and take your life to the next level."

— Seth Greene, Publisher, Founder, Market Domination, LLC

"This book was written for those with self-limiting beliefs and self-doubt."

— Diana Dorell, Bestselling Author of *The Dating Mirror*

"*Freedom at Last!* perfectly restructures the concepts of how we can have true freedom and maximize our potential."

— Frank Shankwitz, Creator and a Founder of the Make-A-Wish Foundation

"This book is both a primer and reminder about the art and science of empowerment."

— David Boufford, Founder of MrPositive.com

"*Freedom at Last!* is a book for all the difference makers out there."

— Shannon Burnett-Gronich, Publicity Expert, Author, and Mother of Three Children

"This book stimulates the imagination of higher achievers, and also appeals to individuals yet to discover themselves."

— Hugh Ballou, Transformational Leadership Strategist, (TM), President of SynerVision® International, Inc.

"*Freedom at Last!* reaffirms the importance of consistency in sustaining your success."

— Nioshi Jackson, Music Producer and Talented Musician

"This book gives an inspiring and insightful look at the secret to lasting personal freedom."

— Penny Zenker, Productivity and Profit Accelerator, TEDx Speaker, Author of *The Productivity Zone,* Strategic Business Coach

"*Freedom at Last!* is for anyone who has struggled to find their 'why' or someone who wants to do something extraordinary."

— J.R. Fenwick, Founder and CEO at FLipThatStock.com

"This book helps you look past the obvious and often unseen while focusing on solutions that will work for you."

— Ari Gronich, Sports Performance Specialist and Bestselling Author

"Many think success is by chance, though *Freedom at Last!* shows you that success is by design."

— Erik Peterson, Music Producer, Singer and Songwriter

"This book tells the story of a helpless immigrant who never gives up, which leads him to become a successful entrepreneur."

— Pas Simpson, Happiness Engineer and Author

"*Freedom at Last!* connects the relationship between success and freedom."

— Steven E. Schmitt, Founder of *The Law of Positivity*

"John's way of explaining the importance and the necessity for getting what you want out of life is not only outstanding, it's inspirational. This country has forgotten how to dream. John reminds us that, not only is it okay to go after what you want, it should be mandatory. This book is a 'must read' for anyone wanting to go to the next level in life."

— Ken Courtright, Producer, Author, Speaker and Founder of 4X Inc.5000 co., Income Store

This book is dedicated to my wife Ruth, and my children, Jude, Precious, Rachel, and Chelsea. They have granted me permission to write this book and supported me during this journey of writing and throughout my career. My family members have been loyal and understanding partners. Without them, this book wouldn't have been possible, and with their support, I have been unstoppable.

Acknowledgments

I extend my gratitude to the following people for supporting me in this journey to success and in helping me to find my voice:

J. R. Fenwick, who has been there for me from the beginning. He believes in me and helped me navigate my entrepreneurial journey. He helped me see beyond myself.

Jeff Hoffman, my friend, my mentor, and inspiration. He sacrificed his time to teach me the practical wisdom of being an entrepreneur.

Dr. George Fraser, another mentor who is always available to listen to me and cry with me "when things get tough."

Berny Dohrmann, my friend, my mentor, my colleague, who insisted I could be an author and that I should "begin writing now!" He helped me see where I could take my organization five years from now and help me make the impossible possible.

The amazing YouSpeakIt Book Program team, who took the time to help me go through the process of writing this book, which would not have been possible without them.

Contents

Introduction

How can you use your unique talents and abilities to create ripple effects in other people's lives?

How you can help others identify who they are born to be and how they can impact people, the community, and the environment?

I wrote this book to help you answer these questions.

In 2001, I came to this country as an immigrant with no relatives, no family, and no role model. Prior to my arrival, I struggled more than ten years through a brutal civil war in Liberia, West Africa. I was not privileged to attend college and start my career like most normal people in America do.

When I arrived in this country, I promised myself and my late father to take advantage of every opportunity to educate myself and help my community. Fifteen years after my settlement in America, I am living that promise. As I have shaped my life, developed myself, and started my own business, I have met thousands of people with great potential.

These people have not experienced half of what I went through in Liberia.

I have:

- Met children and teenagers with bright futures who fail to make a dent in their communities.
- Seen business owners with great experience and knowledge who lean toward quitting their dreams.
- Heard people's stories and backgrounds as they struggled to find their purpose.
- Witnessed the natural abilities and potential of many who could not get off the ground.

I spent sleepless nights thinking of how to share my message with them and with you. Then one day, it dawned on me that I could write a book that touches areas that often appear to be missing in almost everyone I encountered—the young, elderly, employees, solopreneurs, and the entrepreneurs.

There is nothing in this book that you have not heard before. There is no new discovery or phenomena that this book will uncover. I suggest, however, that you begin with an open mind.

After reading each chapter:

- Think about how the chapter applies to your individual situation and circumstances.

- Write one sentence to summarize what you learned.
- Write at least one action step or one thing to apply immediately to your life.

We live in an era of information overload. We are bombarded with many facts and new ideas. I suggest reading this book at least twice to gain the most benefit. I have filled these five chapters with real-life experiences and made them sweet, short, and to the point.

If you are planning to start your own business—if you are an employee, a student, or an entrepreneur—my hope is that you will be able to articulate your *why,* your core reason for doing what you do.

I hope:

- You will be able to get past your inherent, self-limiting beliefs.
- You can see empowerment differently, like a pebble dropped in a pond, creating ripples that help others on their journey to success.
- You define success in your own terms and see the need to give back to the community.

Your success is someone else's miracle.

CHAPTER ONE

The Bigger *Why*

FINDING MY *WHY*

I never dreamed of being a nurse. As a little boy, I always wanted to be an engineer, so I prepared. I pictured myself as an engineer. In my high school courses, I focused on physics and mathematics—classes to help me be an engineer.

Then, something terrible happened. Civil war broke out in my home country, Liberia (West Africa). At that point, my dream to be an engineer fell into shambles. Instead of learning to become an engineer or going to college, I was forced to learn how to survive.

I was forced to learn how to run for my life.

I was forced to help others survive.

I risked my life to save the wounded, the infirmed, and the vulnerable. I witnessed innocent people being killed.

One sunny day in 1996, during the invasion of rebels in Liberia, I vividly remember seeing a young boy shot right in front of me. He was actively bleeding. I immediately took off my shirt and applied pressure on the wound, grabbed the boy, and rushed him to the American Red Cross camp, just a stone's throw from where the boy was injured.

I wondered if we'd survive. My voice was trembling; I held the boy tight.

"Can you save the boy?" I asked as I was laying the boy on the bed.

I was afraid to leave the camp. So, I pleaded to stay with the rescue team because I might not make it home alive. They granted my request. While I was at the camp, I assisted nurses and other medical personnel as they cared for war victims. I was taught basic first-aid skills by the Red Cross. I was unsure about the work I was doing, but I did it anyway, not knowing those skills would form my path in the future.

The Call to Become a Registered Nurse

At the end of the civil war in 2001, I was fortunate to travel to the United States. Upon my arrival, my goal was to go back to school. Immediately, I realized I had no friends, I had no relatives, I had no one to tell me or inform me of what to do. However, I was determined.

I wanted to make a difference in people's lives. I was determined to be an electrical engineer; that was my goal. That was what I believed I was made to be, and I believed that was my calling.

When I rescued that injured boy during the war in Liberia, I received a call. In the camp, I did not realize that was *my* call. I was doing what I loved, naturally, without thinking about it. To me, I was doing what I thought was necessary as a human being—helping.

Injured on the Job

In December 2001, a traumatic experience changed my entire life. About four months after my arrival in the United States, I was working in a meat shop in Washington, DC. I was full of energy, full of life; and I was interacting with the customers on one fateful Saturday afternoon.

Then, one of my coworkers in the shop asked me to cut up a half-dozen chickens for a customer. Without question, I got to work. I cut up the first chicken, the second chicken, the third chicken. Then, on the fourth chicken, something happened—something that changed my life forever, something that I never dreamed would happen, something that I never envisioned coming. I sliced my right thumb with the meat cutter.

I was rushed to the emergency room. I could not believe my eyes. I looked at the doctors in the emergency room.

After immobilizing my right thumb with my left hand, I said, "I lost my thumb! Please save my thumb, please!"

I felt sorry for myself. The physician looked at me and said, "Okay, everything will be fine. We will try our best to save your thumb."

Within hours, I was sent into the pre-operating room, with no one at my side. I had no family, no relatives, no friends, no one to call on, no one to console me but the nurses and the physicians by my side. I was overwhelmed with the stack of papers to sign.

Oh boy, I thought.

"I'm right-handed. How can I sign these papers?" I asked.

"Try your best. Try your left hand," the pre-op nurse said.

She handed me the papers while I painfully signed them all, without understanding what I was signing. However, I trusted and believed the medical staff would do what was best for me.

After this, I was rushed into the operating room, and within hours I was back in the recovery room. I didn't know what to do. All I knew was that my right hand was in a cast, up to the top of my arm. At that point, I was informed that it would be okay; I would be fine.

The second day, after the assessment, they told me I could go home, but to take care of myself. On that fateful day, I had an epiphany. I realized that I needed to give something back. I was very impressed with the care I received. Without a family or any relatives around me, the nursing staff and the physicians gave me competent care—the care that I needed.

Also, they saved my right thumb, which was my main concern. I was so appreciative of their care that I felt that something had to change. I wasn't sure then about changing my career, but I knew that I had to give something back.

Just a Bedside Nurse

Immediately after my recovery—seven months later—I decided that I would go back to school, as I had initially planned when I came to this country. I went to community college, and I enrolled to be a nurse. Eventually, in 2006, I graduated as a registered nurse.

I worked in various aspects of the health care industry. I worked as a medical surgical nurse, a telemetry nurse, a pre-operative nurse, and a psychiatric nurse. But, I was not really satisfied. I felt something was missing. I felt I needed to do more, especially for those who were unable to help themselves. I wanted to help those who go to the hospital and cannot or do not have anyone to advocate for them. I wanted to help those who go back into the community without any empowerment, without anybody supporting them there.

I left my job at the hospital, without knowing what I was going to do. I told my wife that I was going to resign, and that I was going to do something else; I was going to find work that could be fulfilling and make a difference in this life.

Eventually, after I resigned from the hospital, we started a business in 2009 that provided care for the elderly. At that time, we began providing care for the senior population in the community. We were doing medical staffing as well, like a temporary or placement agency. We staffed hospitals and companies locally and across the country. I was passionate to ensure that all our patients were receiving competent care. We advocated for them to be empowered and receive the type of care that I received when I was at the hospital as a patient.

DEFINING YOUR *WHY*

As humans, we all find ourselves doing things that we do not like to do, but we do them anyway. Sometimes we get a job, and we don't know why we took the job.

Sometimes, we focus on how much we're going to make, or paying our bills.

Then, at some point, we each realize that *this is not what I want to do,* and we start feeling burned out. We feel that we are not being fulfilled, because we're doing a job that we don't love.

This is when it is important for you to define your *why*—your prime motivation and passion in life—and to understand your core reasons for doing what you do.

The Challenges of Defining Your *Why*

When we choose a job as we are growing up, we often plan to do something that we love. Maybe you were influenced by your parents or by friends, or sometimes social or academic scenes influenced what you wanted to do. Then, you went to school with the notion of finding a job, or doing something that would pay the bills or make more money.

I challenge you to look at the reason why you do what you do.

Are you doing what you really love to do?

You may not know the exact reason for feeling pulled in a certain direction. However, at some point, this challenge should result in a shift to finding a job that you love to do. It will eventually cause you to define your reasons for choosing your work.

At a minimum, it may result in dissatisfaction and regret.

How I Was Able to Identify My *Why*

As mentioned at the onset, I always wanted to be an engineer. Now, I look at different experiences while I was back home in Liberia and look at what I am doing now with new understanding. When we started the business in 2009, I wasn't thinking about why I was doing what I was doing.

Then one night, I was having trouble sleeping, and I was thinking about the effect of the work we were doing, and how it impacted my life.

I was thinking: *Is the money worth my time, or is it in the happiness and fulfillment I identify and find my why?*

One day, I received a call from a woman whose father, a man who had been in our care, recently died. She explained to us how she appreciated the care we provided for her dad and how it had made the transition of her father smooth and comfortable. At that point, I identified and proved to myself the reason why I do what I do, and I could identify my *why*. Looking at the experiences of those people we provided care for, it was obvious to me that what we did truly impacted their lives.

My *Why* Drives Everything I Do

You may be working at a job that you hate—many people are. We only look at the end results of a job—we look at how much money we are going to receive from the work. There are times, as professionals, when we don't feel like doing anything after we wake up in the morning. We want to do other things instead of going to work.

When that happens to me, I think about who will benefit from my work:

- People who are sick
- People who need our care
- People who are stressed out
- People who are worried about someone providing care for them

Those thoughts give me a drive in terms of what I do and my duty. I'm able to identify my *why* any time that I'm stressed out—either from the job, from the office, or whatever I do. I always think about my drive to help. That motivation drives every task I do—either a patient assessment, a patient visit, or providing care. I am driven when I think about the impact that I have on people's lives.

Identifying your *why* is of the utmost importance in everything that you do. I don't know why or what drives you. Sometimes you might feel stressed, tired, or that you are not being fulfilled in everything that you do.

The first thing that you need to find is the answer to a question.

How do you make a difference in people's lives?

Most of the people who are successful today know the importance of their *why*. The first thing I ask you to do is to identify that *why*. Identify the importance of that drive that makes you wake up every morning and do what you love to do.

FINDING YOUR *WHY*

Everything in life is a process. Finding your *why* is the same. For some people, it's easy for them to identify. For some, it can be challenging. But if you understand the process, you know how to go about it. Then, I tell you, finding your *why* is as easy as learning your ABCs.

Identifying What You Love to Do

The first step is to identify what you love to do. That means that you must find out what it is that keeps you going, what it is that *gets* you going. You should identify what people call your strengths, or your *gut feeling,* or whatever you want to call it. After you identify what you love to do, then do it over and over.

People will see you, and they will know that you love what you do. They will see it in the way you're doing your work. And *you* will be able to see and feel it in your work.

The second way to identify your *why* is to find what you can do without giving it a second thought. If someone were to call you up, for instance, at two o' clock in the morning, you could do it without batting an eye, as they say. You wouldn't need to stop to decide whether you should go. That is your *why,* and that is the first step in knowing exactly what you love to do.

At some point, you may look at what you love to do, and think: *Well, this is what I love to do. However, it does not translate to income for me.*

Well, it depends on how you look at it, or the way it has been defined. Being fulfilled, or doing what you love to do, does not necessarily *have* to translate into income, although there's nothing wrong with that.

But at the same time, loving what you do does not necessarily translate into the question: *How much money am I going to make from doing what I love to do?*

Aligning Your *Why* With Your Values

Value is defined as something that you believe in, something that always holds true to you. Some people define it as your integrity.

What gets you going?

What is it that, no matter what, always holds true, all the time?

For instance, what if you're going to a convenience store with your friends, and they ask you to take a candy and put it in your pocket without paying for it?

Would you do that?

Does that align with your values?

Would you do that just because your friends asked you to do it?

Or would you not do it because honesty is the best policy?

When you know your values, everything else you do will revolve around that, including your *why*.

A few years ago, I was assigned to perform an initial consultation assessment for a potential client. The family was requesting a nursing visit every day, seven days a week. When I went for the assessment, I realized that the potential client did not really need daily visits. All she needed was one visit a month.

I know my core value is to be honest and to make sure that the client receives appropriate services. So, I recommended that instead of visits every day—which, of course, would result in more income for the company—we do just one visit a month, and that if any issue or anything came up with the client, we could increase the frequency based on the client's condition.

The family appreciated my recommendation, and we saved her lots of money. At the same time, I felt fulfilled because we did not provide care without looking at what would be the best thing for the family and for that client. We received lots of referrals from the family a few months later.

So, aligning one's values goes go a long way in becoming fulfilled and happy. People will appreciate you if you hold yourself to your own values.

Ensuring That You Live by Your Purpose

When you wake up in the morning, you may ask yourself questions like these:

- *Why am I here?*
- *What is my purpose for living?*

- *Was I born to go to school, graduate from school, find a job, work, raise a family, and die?*
- *Why was I made?*

Sometimes we think about that, and eventually—maybe after a few years—one dies, or something major happens. These questions can be a revolving cycle, and most people find it difficult to find the purpose of their life, to find the reason they came into existence. Yet, they want to know.

Work to understand why you came into existence, and how what you do makes an impact in this life. When you realize that, when you know that, and you live by that purpose, you can live a fulfilled life, and be happy in what you do.

The purpose of finding your *why,* understanding exactly what it is, can be daunting or a little bit challenging. Finding what you love to do and aligning that purpose—why you do what you do—will pull you toward your true path. It will also ensure that you live by that purpose all the time.

At times, you may fall off the path because of an insult or because of events that occur in your life. Sometimes, you fall completely off the cliff! But if you continue to live by your purpose and live by your *why,* then you've ensured that you will be fulfilled in everything that you do in your life.

CHAPTER TWO

Be Who You Want to Be

SELF-LIMITING BELIEFS

Many people today like to achieve their goals and want to be somebody *great* in the future. Unfortunately, most of us use our background or situation as an excuse for not being able to succeed. The excuse that most people make is inherent in what I call *self-limiting* beliefs.

Ask yourself these questions:

- *Have I ever been in a meeting with others and found I was afraid of sharing new ideas?*
- *Have I ever allowed others to decide for me because I doubted myself?*
- *Have I ever shied away from an opportunity because I questioned my abilities or knowledge?*

If you answered yes to two or more of these questions, you are a self-doubter. Simply stated, you have what I would diagnose as a self-limiting belief.

What is a self-limiting belief?

Although we may have beliefs about our abilities, our rights, our duties, and so on, self-limiting beliefs are how we *feel* about ourselves—our self-identities—about other people, or about the world in general.

Bruce Frankel, author of *What Should I Do with the Rest of My Life,* says, "Self-limiting beliefs are everywhere, in a part of all of us, to a greater or lesser degree." Simply put, we all suffer—at some point in our lives—from this self-inflicted disease. Frankel continues, "The key to overcoming many of these are understanding how we got them, and then banishing them through sustained activities."

Let's consider how dangerous self-limiting beliefs are.

Self-Limiting Beliefs Can Kill Your Dreams

As mentioned earlier, self-limiting beliefs are a self-inflicted disease. This is a chronic disease, a problem, that is often triggered by our environment or some sort of pain we've experienced in the past.

When I was working at the facility a few years ago, we admitted a patient for a suicide attempt. She was in her mid-twenties. When I was conducting my assessment, I kept asking myself why a very young woman, who is vibrant, attempted to commit suicide. We needed to identify the cause of her suicide attempt so that she could be safely discharged.

We did inquire. She had experienced an unsuccessful relationship two years prior, and she promised herself not to ever go into any other relationship. Then, she found she was not attracted to the opposite sex, or anyone. She became withdrawn and isolated, which eventually led her to feeling unwanted. Next, she attempted to poison herself.

Your situation might not be as extreme as this young woman's. But isn't that what happens when you work at a job you hate?

Instead of feeling fulfilled, you slowly kill yourself.

Self-Limiting Beliefs Cause Future Problems

Self-limiting beliefs are dream-killers.

Have you ever thought of a good idea or a vision when you were younger, then as you grew older, somebody talked you out of your dreams?

Why do you often talk yourself out of great ideas?

Continuing this path of self-limitation can lead to dangerous and bigger problems in the future. In addition to the lack of fulfillment in your life, self-limiting beliefs can cause bigger health problems as well. Your feelings and emotions, once experienced, can produce chemical changes in your brains and body.

Do you remember how you feel when you finish exercising or working out?

Do you remember the rush of happiness when you received a good grade on a test?

Your brain releases a chemical called *dopamine,* a neurotransmitter that controls that path of emotion. On the other hand, when you feel unfulfilled and sad, the body inhibits the release of a chemical called *serotonin,* a neurotransmitter that is responsible for the feeling of well-being, the feeling of being fulfilled. Going down a path of multiple self-limiting beliefs, not doing what you love to do, can lead to regret, self-condemnation, and depression.

Also, self-limiting beliefs affect your productivity. If you continue working at a job you hate, your productivity will decrease with time. This decline may result in your underachievement and lead to not being promoted.

PEOPLE WITH SELF-LIMITING BELIEFS

As mentioned previously, we all suffer from this self-limiting malady at some point in our lives. All great leaders of our time experienced some sort of self-doubt, from Oprah Winfrey to Steve Jobs. But what set these leaders apart is that they never dwelt in self-doubt.

If you have self-limiting beliefs, you need not beat yourself up. Many people—great people of our time—had these beliefs, and they were able to overcome them eventually.

How I Developed Self-Limiting Beliefs

A few years ago, I was relating the experience I had in the civil war in Liberia, in West Africa. A friend of mine was inspired by my story, and said, "This is a unique story, John. I think others need to hear about this."

That was the first time I ever thought of writing a book. I never considered myself an author. I thought about this for years—two years, to be precise. Then, I began writing. I wrote about one hundred pages, then I stopped.

I kept asking myself: *Who will read my book? Will the book sell? How will I go about writing this book?*

Self-limiting beliefs set in, and I stopped listening to my soul. I wrote my book in under two years, then I stopped. Then everywhere I'd go, I thought about my business.

The message I always received was: *You are an expert in the homecare industry. Do you have a book?*

Everybody would tell me this. Instead of being excited, I'd always find ways to talk myself out of being an author.

It came to a point in my life where I thought: *Maybe something is wrong with me. Seriously, maybe I need a psychiatric evaluation. Maybe I need to have someone look at me in the mirror.*

So, I did the next best thing. I looked to the people in my inner circle who are highly successful. I interviewed these people to identify if they experienced similar situations about not wanting to do what they loved to do, or not wanting to write a book, or not wanting to become who they wanted to be.

I wanted to know if they had ever felt the way I was feeling. At this point, I needed to know if the way I was feeling was normal.

J. R. Fenwick

The first person I interviewed was Mr. Fenwick. Mr. Fenwick is an author who has started several businesses. He is currently the CEO of the company called Flip That Stock, a web-based tutorial program.

When he was in seventh grade, he knew he wanted to have his own business. He started a paper route business while in school, then he started a lawn-cutting service as well. He really wanted to be his own boss. Then, as often happens to us when we are young, Mr. Fenwick's parents wanted him to become something else. They wanted him to be a medical doctor or a nurse, because that was the family's trade. Self-limiting beliefs set in. Mr. Fenwick settled for the path his parents set for him.

He thought: *I cannot start my own business. I need to work for others so I can survive.*

He talked himself out of his own dreams.

Steve Gurney

Steve Gurney is a businessman who owns a publishing company that distributes resource books to all hospitals and facilities in the mid-Atlantic region. The idea of publishing resource books came to him when his grandfather was looking for a nursing home placement. He was looking for books that listed nursing homes in the Washington metro area, but he could not find any.

He decided to start publishing resource books for seniors. At the time, Mr. Gurney did not have any savings or money in the bank. He went from bank to bank looking for loans, all to get a line of credit to start his publishing business, but to no avail. At the same time, his girlfriend, whom he depended on, broke up with him. Self-limiting beliefs set in.

He thought: *Maybe this is not for me.*

Again, he talked himself out of his own dream.

As you can see, none of us is immune to self-limiting beliefs. These doubts happen to everyone, no matter who we are. We let people talk us out of our dreams or what we love to do. We also talk ourselves out of our own dreams.

Recognize that these self-limiting beliefs can affect and impede your success. Learn to identify this common process so that these beliefs cannot prevent you from becoming who you wanted to be.

OVERCOMING YOUR SELF-LIMITING BELIEFS

Remember this phrase: *Begin with the end in mind.*

Defining your purpose ties in with identifying your *why*. If you know what you want to be five, ten, fifteen, or twenty years from now—if you know the reason you are in existence—this reality will help you overcome your self-limiting beliefs.

Why You Came Into Existence

Everything and everyone in this life came into existence for a reason. I call this your *life purpose*. Whatever you do—your goals, your mission—must align with your purpose. Your life is like a beam; it must be balanced. When goals do not align with your purpose in life, self-limiting beliefs set in. Your hopes and dreams never manifest into results.

There are three steps that will help you to identify your purpose and overcome self-limiting beliefs:

1. **Define your purpose.** Find out what you want. This could be your goals, your objectives, or the outcome you would love to achieve.

2. **Identify strong reasons why you need to pursue step one.** The stronger your reasons to pursue something, the greater motivation you will have in pursuing it. Thus, the more results you achieve.

3. **Develop the motivation and willingness to make necessary changes.** For this to occur, your why must be clear and well-defined. This may take some time for you to figure out, but it is necessary if you really want to make a shift.

As it is often said, "Motivation beats meditation."

Positive quotes and inspiring words on a refrigerator magnet will only go so far. To move forward, you need to get out of your own way, for the most part.

A few years ago, I went for a physical. I received a follow-up call the week after my appointment. I immediately knew that something wasn't right and asked for an appointment. The next day, I was at my doctor's office.

He reviewed lab results while I waited impatiently. "Everything looks great," he said, "but . . ."

Yes, I was waiting for the *but*. That is what this follow-up appointment was all about. I leaned forward, paying as much attention as I could.

He said, "Your hemoglobin A1C is a little bit high. You may be pre-diabetic."

I couldn't believe my ears! I never dreamt of being diabetic.

As a nurse, I knew the disease process of diabetics, so I asked a profound question. "What should I do? Prescriptions?"

He looked at me and said, "I think you are getting ahead of yourself, don't you?"

I nodded.

He said, "You have two options. Low-dose glipizide, or exercise."

Of course, I preferred doing exercise to taking any medicines. Prior to that, my workout program had been hit-or-miss and erratic, but after that conversation with my doctor, my *why* went up.

I immediately stopped making all the excuses for not having a workout program, such as: The weather is too hot. It's too cold. I don't feel like it today.

I made all the necessary changes because my life depended on it.

Isn't that true with our purpose, our life, and our mission in life? Making a change is a conscious decision. You must decide to change without any reservation.

Identifying Your Strengths

Strength can be defined as:

- Ability to withstand pressure
- Being physically strong
- Quality that allows one to deal with problems in a determined and effective way

The latter definition was true for Albert Einstein. He failed a French exam but was determined to find his strength in physics, not language.

The latter definition was true when J. K. Rowling realized how disorganized she was but focused on storytelling skills to write Harry Potter instead of becoming more organized and orderly.

One of the most important parts of ultimately defining your purpose is to find your strengths—what you are good at.

When I was not able to write my book, I was thinking that something was missing in me. I believed that I needed to find I was good at it, what I loved to do, my strength. I found this search difficult initially. I spoke to many people who could see me for who I was. I spoke to people who knew more about me, who could see my reaction, who could see how and what I do daily.

What most people saw in me was someone who loved to have an impact on people's lives, someone who loved to see others be successful, and someone who loved to care for the elderly. I went into a denial state for almost four years, until I began focusing on my strength of impacting people's lives. I realized what my strength is, and I focused on it.

Mr. Fenwick took a different route at identifying his strengths. He graduated as a pre-med nurse from Hampton University in Virginia. He did a bit of bedside nursing, then worked at a corporate job. He realized during his career path that his greatest strengths are speaking and system set-up. He maximized this strength, and now owns a multi-million-dollar company.

Mr. Gurney wasn't sure what he wanted to do when he graduated from college. He had a humble beginning and was broke. He found his strength was helping other seniors find livable places. He honed the space and leveraged the opportunity.

There are three steps to helping you find your strengths.

1. **Seek feedback.** Identify people from your inner circle who can help you find what you are good at: ask them to consider your qualities, your personality, and so on.

2. **Find common themes.** Based on the feedback from the first step, look for trends—what do most people think you are good at?

3. **Activate your strengths.** Maximize them and put them to work for you.

Ways to Prevent Self-Limiting Beliefs

Beliefs affect our day-to-day activities and decisions. Most of all, they affect our utmost potential. The fact that you are successful does not necessarily mean you are free from self-limiting beliefs, because preventing self-limiting beliefs is a continual process.

Self-limiting beliefs are like a fever. Your body temperature has a physiological impact on your well-being. A fever is your body's response to infection, trying to kill invading pathogens and sometimes acting as a warning sign for imminent danger. Self-limiting beliefs are the mind's response to pathogenic thoughts—and they act as warning signs of imminent danger to our progress, success, or true potential. Your goal is to keep yourself at optimal temperature with total and complete control.

To prevent and let go of your self-limiting beliefs, there are three things you need to do:

1. **Identify:** Self-limiting beliefs can be based on *assumptions*—what you never experienced, or on *facts*—what you have experienced, such as a divorce, an auto accident, or loss of a job. If your beliefs are based on facts—on what has happened to you—they can be treated as problems that have solutions. You will have to solve these problems to clear a path to your success.

2. **Probe:** Ask a series of questions that bring the problem to light. The more questions you ask, the more clarity you have regarding your self-limiting beliefs. Some of the questions to ask are:

    - *How did I come to form this belief?*

- ○ *Why have I maintained this belief?*
- ○ *What am I saying to myself?*
- ○ *Why can't I overcome this challenge?*

3. **Pleasure:** Focus on the benefits of letting go of your self-limiting beliefs. Think with the end in mind:

    - ○ *Will you have more freedom by overcoming self-limiting beliefs?*
    - ○ *Will it increase your bottom line?*
    - ○ *Will it give you more time with your family and friends?*

Thinking and mediating on the benefits of busting self-limiting beliefs will give you the results that you want.

CHAPTER THREE

Making a Difference

DEFINING STRESS AND PAIN

Have you ever thought of an impactful organization, group, or individual and wondered: *How do they do that?*

About a year ago, I had a lunch with a man in Alexandria, Virginia, who happened to be a professor at George Mason University. He mentioned how he turned the law school around and attracted many people to enroll. He believed his success was due to keeping his goal—making a difference in people's lives—in the front of his mind.

Why is that so important?

Why do we need to make a difference in people's lives?

How can we do the same?

In our organization, members of our senior population usually prefer to stay in their own homes, stress free. One of our core competencies is identifying and helping our clients—or *our family,* as we call them—identify their needs and how our services can meet those needs.

To make a difference in people's lives, you must be able to identify their needs. This is your first step.

What Causes Stress

Stress occurs when our problems or circumstances lack a solution. In my world of providing care for the elderly and their loved ones, one of the key components of what we do is identifying the *insults,* or the cause, of the problem. This approach is not unique to the medical industry; it is applicable to all businesses. However, to understand what causes stress, we need to know exactly what stress is.

Simply put, stress is a primarily physical response to a dire situation or circumstance. When stressed, the body thinks it's under attack and releases a complex mix of hormones, such as adrenaline, to prepare the body for physical action.

In my experience dealing with caregivers, the release of this hormone brings them to the point of asking for our services. For instance, a patient has two falls within days due to confusion or delirium. Or, a patient wandered off due to dementia and was found by police. After something like this happens, we receive calls from caregivers, usually the children of the patient.

Identifying what gives people stress and at what point they would need our services or product is the key to our success.

Stress Recognition

Identifying and recognizing a stressful situation and how to respond to it is important as well. As a professional, experienced service provider or business owner, you should be able to identify a situation from having encountered it before. Then, you acknowledge its existence and validate its reality. When you recognize and provide feedback, you reassure the individual who needs your professional help.

Complications of Stressful Situations

The next component is identifying complications related to the present situation or the problem you are about to solve.

Identify the worst-case scenario: *What could happen if this situation worsens at all?*

For example, when a family requests services to care for a parent with multiple falls, we need to understand the complications of falls—the senior could have fractured a hip, needed a hip replacement, and developed other complications due to surgical procedures, and so on.

For the caregiver who cares for Mom at home, they may develop high blood pressure and other complications related to the stress of giving constant care. This stress may result in a strained relationship.

Creating a list and helping your client recognize potential problems or challenges sets you apart from other providers. Also, it helps you prepare for additional needs that your clients might develop in the future. The list helps you to prepare to help them in the long run.

These initial steps of defining the stress and pain are very important while you are planning or starting up a business. For those who are already in business, it is important that you define the stress and pain your clients undergo so that you make changes over time. Reviewing this over and over will help you focus on what to hone, what to concentrate on to better help and assist your clients.

STRESS ASSESSMENT

Assessing the problem is the initial step of any situation or problem. Any successful business or organization consciously goes through this process. This is true in the field of medicine, engineering, or any other discipline.

Imagine going to your doctor.

Upon arrival, your physician looks at you, says, "Since you have come to visit me today, I'm going to write you a prescription for pain relief."

Suppose this happens without assessing the reason you actually came for the visit—without checking your vital signs, checking your blood pressure, and making sure that you are okay. Without looking for the problem, a wrong diagnosis could be made and whatever treatment is prescribed may be useless.

Assessing the situation will help you and your clients to know how to better deal with the situation at hand.

Diagnosis Identification

It is often said, "A problem identified is a problem half solved."

Diagnosis is a medical term that often means illness or symptom identification. It may mean problem identification, problem recognition, or problem discovery. This is true with every adventure you can imagine. Every organization was formed as the result of a problem that was discovered and diagnosed.

For instance, the Wright brothers identified the need for an aircraft that could steer and maneuver. Hence, they invented the first controllable airplane. Steve Jobs saw the need to invent a readily accessible, affordable, user-friendly, handheld device—in this case, a smartphone. Hence, his company invented iPhones and other small, portable devices.

The list goes on and on, but the point is clear. You must identify and clearly diagnose problems you would like to solve to be successful in any endeavor.

When we were starting our in-home care business, we went through a similar process of identifying the *bigger* problems we could solve. We noticed that many of our clients were aging and would need help at some point with issues as they age. Because of discovering, properly identifying, and diagnosing this problem, we were able to begin our business.

Prognosis Identification

The second step in assessing stress is to ask yourself: *Will this problem continue? Is this a short-term or long-term process?*

We call these questions *disease process,* or *prognosis.* Prognosis simply means predicting the unfolding of events. The Wright brothers knew that the invention of controllable air travel was not a short-term problem. People continue to have the need to travel from one point to another. Their invention has been so refined that the airline business continues to be a multi-billion-if not trillion-dollar, business today. The same process applies to iPhones and other smartphone inventions. People continue to have a need for smarter and easier-to-use devices.

A long-term problem requires a long-term solution. For a company to sustain and outlast its competitors, it needs to predict or know the prognosis or problem it is trying to solve. This step is important and cannot be overlooked. In our area of business, we have identified that providing care for the elderly population—in most cases, unfortunately—is a long-term prognosis.

An active, elderly man fell and broke his hip, went for surgical procedure, recovered after surgery, and was discharged home. As we predicted, it turned out that this man needed additional services after recovery, and at his age, it was very hard.

Through this unfortunate example, we saw this need, and now we also know that prior to venturing into any business endeavors, we need to be able to provide a combination of both short-term and long-term solutions.

Stress Identication

Once you have successfully provided accurate diagnosis and prognosis of the problem you are trying to solve, the next step is to identify what is most stressful to the client or clients you are about to assist. Unfortunately, most business owners – specifically the new startups – often miss this step. While they talk about the features of their services or products, they fail to identify what their clients really want.

When we started our company, Prestige Health Care Resources, we traveled back and forth between cities and states. We did a lot of marketing presentations; however, our return on those efforts was very low. We wondered what we were doing wrong. We knew there were a lot of people looking for our services.

Why was the phone not ringing?

It took six years for us to figure out what the issue was. We had not dedicated enough time to properly identify and define our clients' *pain point,* asking what was most stressful to them. After we identified this piece, our phone started ringing, and has continued to ring ever since.

Conscious and intentional assessment of the stress of the client population you are planning to serve is the key to every successful endeavor. In short, make sure you have mastered this technique.

Keep in mind that these three steps are the initial steps of this process.

Every business startup and every business owner must:

1. Diagnose the problem.
2. Identify your prognosis.
3. Identify the stress that your clients are going through, or the problem that you are trying to solve for your clients.

RELIEF FOR CLIENTS

At some point in our lives, we all experience pain. You have experienced pain, too.

How did you feel when that pain was abated?

Can you still remember what helped you and how you were able to find relief for your pain or stressful situation?

Relief is an alleviation, ease, or deliverance through the removal of pain, anxiety, distress, or oppression of any kind. Simply put, relief is a state of the reduction or removal of something unpleasant. To provide relief is an *act,* an intentional approach that requires action on your part.

Every business—either a startup or an experienced process—knows and will have a process that defines their products or services that provide relief.

I have developed three ways to identify your clients' pain:

- Build a solution system.
- Be a magnet.
- Educate, enlighten, empower.

Let's consider them one at a time.

Build a Solution System

How do you provide relief for your client?

First, you need to know and understand the people you are interacting with. You need to perceive what I call *identity attributes.* This is necessary because every client is unique, and every situation is unique. However, specific clients could be clustered based on the most frequent problem or stress that needs to be solved. In our organization, we often use the acronym KYC, or *Know Your Client,* as the process of identifying unique client or patient needs in order to provide appropriate relief.

A few years ago, we received a call from a family member asking us what she needed to do after her mom got home from rehab. With our KYC process in place, we initially informed her that we needed to conduct a specific assessment with Mom, we needed to review a care plan with the discharge planner, and then we needed to assess the home environment to ensure safety. This process has helped us proactively solve many problems in a timely and effective manner.

You can do the same. Successful companies must have some sort of process or system in place to ensure any stressful encounter is solved in a timely fashion. The fact that you provide a stepwise approach will always provide immediate relief to your client.

Be the Magnet

You cannot be the source of solutions to everyone, because you cannot do it all. You cannot be a jack-of-all-trades. Avoid this pitfall if you really want to be successful. We learned this the hard way as a startup. We wanted to convert every call for help into clients even if their need was not in our sweet spot—the specific market we served best. We immediately realized that instead of being the solution to every client's stressful problems—that is, their pain point—we could become a company of magnetic attraction.

One of the properties of magnets is their power of attraction. Another unique benefit of magnets is the ability to guide people when lost, as in a compass. To provide relief for the population you serve—your clients, your potential customers—you must be the guide, or the one providing direction and guidance.

Now, when we receive a call and the theme is not our sweet spot, we refer to other companies who are experts and better able to find solutions to the problems.

We became a referral compass, so to speak. Initially, we thought we were giving away business. However, we also started receiving referrals from the companies we referred to. We even went so far as to make follow-up calls to potential clients, to ensure the people we referred them to were able to solve their problems. This kept us in their mind always. They called us for different kinds of problems and situations, and we provided as much direction as we could.

Being able to find and identify resources for potential clients provides immediate relief for them and for you. When you refer them to other people, you experience a sense of fulfillment. You feel you have made a difference in people's lives. When people feel that you are resourceful, they tend to contact you whenever they have any problem. You become the magnet, the compass, and the guide for them.

Educate, Enlighten, and Empower

Finding and identifying long-term problems to solve is your key to success. When you have been able to identify one problem to solve, you become the solution person. You become the go-to company or person. You have all the clients you could ever imagine.

Is that the end of it all?

No. To maintain or create value you must remember and follow these three *Es*:

1. **Educate.** Educating your client about products or services you provide enables them to be well informed. There are so many ways you can do this. The most common educational vehicles are: web postings, tutorials, blogs, online manuals, or monthly manuals.
2. **Enlighten.** When a client receives educational material or content from you, they become enlightened about the solution or approach to their problem. They have greater knowledge or understanding about a subject or situation.
3. **Empower.** To empower means to give authority or to grant the permission to do something. Any time you provide educational material through a medium of your choice, your client becomes enlightened, and the result is empowerment. This allows them to be drawn to you like a magnet, instead of being repelled by you. The next time they have a problem, guess who they will be looking for? You.

Most successful companies know this. They know value creation is the key to your lasting relationship with your client. You always want to provide relief and peace of mind to your clients, even if you must go the extra mile.

If you are thinking of starting your own business, or you already have a business, think about how you make a difference in people's lives, and design a reproducible system to catapult you and your business to a greater trajectory.

CHAPTER FOUR

The Power of Empowerment

DEFINING EMPOWERMENT

> *Incredible change appears in your life when you decide to take control of what you do have power over instead of craving control over what you do not.*
>
> ~ Steve Maraboli

Let's investigate your relationship with power:

- What do you have power over?
- What do you want to take control of?
- What do you want to let go?

Many of us know that to be successful, we must learn how to empower others. If you want to be successful, truly successful, you must learn to *let go* by empowering others.

I cannot say this better than Bill George, who said, "The role of leaders is not to get other people to follow them, but to empower others to lead."

Whom are you leading?

Whom are you empowering?

John Maxwell rightfully said, "If you are leading without a follower, you are just taking a walk."

Let's look at the definition of empowerment.

What Is Empowerment?

We need to establish what empowerment really means. The word empowerment has been loosely used in various settings and industries. It could have a different meaning to different people and organizations. However, for this book we will focus on how it relates to you as an individual and business owner.

I define empowerment as a social process that helps individuals gain control. Empowerment fosters power for people to take control of their own lives and their community by acting on issues they deem important. Empowerment changes one's assumptions about power, helping, and succeeding.

Do you notice that the word empowerment at its core has the word *power?*

To fully understand how to empower people, you need to understand two things about power.

1. Empowerment requires the knowledge that power can change. If power cannot change, then empowerment is not possible. The concept of power in empowerment often relates to our ability to make others do what we want. To make others do what we want, relationships must be built. Power is exchanged from you to the individual you trust. This power can be in the form of authority, responsibility, and so on.

2. Second, empowerment requires expansion of power. For some, the concept of power expansion may not come to mind at first. If you have an authority and power that you are not willing to share with others, this makes you a powerful but selfish person who will never grow beyond their own nose, so to speak. Power remains in the hands of the powerful unless they share.

How do you share or expand power?

By inspiring others. When you empower others, you expand both in capability and ability.

Ways to Empower Yourself

Empowerment starts from within. You cannot give someone power or authority if you do not have it. In addition, to empower others, you must know yourself.

According to Tina Lifford, "When you know yourself, you are empowered. When you accept yourself, you are invisible."

How do you know yourself?

By self-examination or finding an accountability partner. If you feel that you need to be empowered—which we all do at some point in our lives—you may want to switch your perspective and choose to believe that you are *not* powerless or stuck. No matter what is holding you back, you can make necessary changes and needed adjustments.

Accepting yourself means knowing your limitations, your strengths, and your weaknesses. It means knowing what you can give and what you cannot give.

There are three simple ways to help you change your perspective from disempowered to empowered:

1. **Change your limiting beliefs and fears.** Get into the habit of challenging and questioning any self-limiting beliefs, doubts, and fears.

2. **Reinforce your strengths and abilities.** Frequent affirmation that you are powerful and strong goes a long way. Build yourself up with encouraging words and thoughts.

3. **Take action.** Willingness to act when necessary builds your confidence and morale. Take small action steps and celebrate every success along the way.

How to Empower Others

Have you found yourself in a situation, such as calling your utility company about an incorrect bill sent to you?

The customer service representative bends over backward, so to speak, to right the wrong and make necessary changes. This situation occurs when an employee is given permission or empowered to give priority to customer care.

How can you empower others?

If you are a parent, how can you empower your child or children?

For many, empowering others might be challenging. However, the process starts with nurturing an environment of trust and reliability.

There are five things you need to know if you really want to empower others:

1. **Be liberal with information.** Providing and sharing important information will allow the individual to make decision in your absence. And of course, people live by example. Do not be like a travel agent who tells people about places they've never been themselves.

2. **Provide concise and specific expectations.** To empower others, make sure your expectations and objectives are clear. This clarity will guide the individual being empowered to make decisions.

3. **Permit mistakes.** You must foster an environment in which you allow others to make mistakes. The first time you empower someone to make decisions, it will not be perfect. If they make mistakes, use that as an opportunity to train and teach without reprimanding.

4. **Celebrate accomplishments.** We all need encouragement, so does the individual you are empowering. Every accomplishment made—no matter how little it is—must be recognized, praised, and celebrated. This boosts the individual's morale and reinforces positive behavior.

5. **Encourage a learning environment.** Empowerment is an ongoing process. Empowering others is like releasing a spiral spring, it must be in an environment where it's gradually released until it can stand by itself. Individuals must be in an environment where they can continue to learn and be supported.

Empowering others is an ongoing process; it takes time, effort, and energy. Ensure the individual you are empowering is a good fit. Do not dump responsibility or authority on someone if you cannot confirm their strengths or abilities. Assure your expectations and theirs are aligned.

EMPOWERMENT SUSTAINABILITY

We all want to maintain what we have. Fifteen years ago, I bought my first car. I was so excited, as it was truly a huge milestone for me at the time. Then, the car broke down. The technician at the shop linked the car breakdown to a lack of maintenance, not servicing the car as recommended. It cost me a fortune at the time to fix the car. It wouldn't have cost me a fortune if I had learned how to maintain and sustain it. I needed a plan and system in place to service the car as recommended.

Isn't that true with empowerment?

To sustain empowerment, it must be maintained. It must be nourished. In the next few pages, we will discuss three frameworks of empowerment sustainability.

Internal Focus

For you to grow, you must be willing to empower others. However, to empower others, you must determine what type of future you would like to build for yourself.

Who do you want to be part of that future?

Assess who could be part of your future goals or dreams. If you have an organization or your own company with employees, determine individual unique talents and skills and see if they resonate with yours before committing time, energy, and resources in empowering the individual.

Collaborating with your team is essential at this juncture. It means you must outline your goals, mission, and vision. These three must be shared with any individual you want to empower. You will also want to discuss how success and accomplishment will be measured.

Identifying Ways to Empower Yourself—External Focus

> *Lacking an external focus, the mind turns inward on itself and creates problems to solve, even if the problems are undefined or unimportant. If you find a focus, an ambitious goal that seems impossible and forces you to grow, these doubts disappear.*
>
> ~ Steve Ferris
> *The 4-Hour Workweek*

You need to find a focus, an external focus. This means finding resources you will need to bridge or cover your weaknesses.

Educate yourself and learn from others. Identify areas for growth so that you can empower others. You cannot give what you do not have. I cannot not empower you or teach you how to play piano if I have never played one before. If you want to empower your team to be pianists, you must at least have a basic education and the skills to play piano.

If you lack the skills you need to empower others, you may consider finding external resources to train the individuals. It is important to identify the training and technical supports to deliver what is needed.

Identify and invest in appropriate technology. We live in the world of technology. Believe it or not; it's here to stay. To maintain sustainability, you need to invest in technology that will help you to grow as you empower your team. There are many software options you could use to help put a system or process in place. Identify the one that works for you and stick with it.

I cannot say it better than W. Edwards Deming, "If you cannot describe what you are doing as a process, you don't know what you are doing."

Empowering people is a process. It's an intentional process; you cannot leave it to chance. If you have a good system and process in place, it will shorten your way to success and shorten the road to reaching your goals.

Culmination

When I say *culmination,* I mean reaching or maximizing your highest potential.

How can you reach a culminate level of your career, your business, or your goals?

By empowering others: your people, your family, and anyone around you who can help you reach your goals.

To attain this height of greatness, you must ensure that your team is striving, growing, and looking for ways to become great as well. The same applies to you. You must be willing to grow. You can only become great if those surrounding you are great and winners.

How do you know if those surrounding you are winners or great people?

One way is by making a list of those surrounding you, analyzing each person to identify if they are truly helping you to grow. Ask yourself if they are truly helping you reach your highest potential. If they are, empower them; if they are not, look for new circle of people and influence. A few years ago, we did this exercise within our organization. We really wanted to empower our staff so we could reach the culminate level.

We know we must do what Bryant McGill said, "When you are not willing to be challenged, disturbed or offended, you are not willing to explore your weaknesses or ever reach your highest potential."

We were willing to challenge the status quo and challenge we did! After our self-appraisal, we realized only 30 percent of our employees were empower-able. We devoted our efforts and built systems to empower those who were ready for it. The rest, we gracefully let go. It has been the best decision we ever made as an organization. Try it and you will see the difference in the growth in yourself or your organization.

BE THE CHEERLEADER

> *Great things in business are never done by one person, they are done by a team of people.*
>
> ~ Steve Jobs

Building a winning team is essential to achieving your goals and dreams. To be this successful team builder, you must be a great cheerleader. Great companies have great cheerleaders who build a winning team.

How can you be a great cheerleader?

How can you build a winning team?

Let's consider three things successful companies have in common.

The Act of Positivity

A farmer sold produce. He had a store, and people came in and purchased food items. All his employees were portrayed as happy because they kept smiles on their faces. They had lots of customers, and all their customers assumed their business was great and very successful. All the employees, including the owner, wore a label, a badge, with the inscription: *Life is good.*

This label always sparked a conversation with new customers: "How's life good on your side of town? What does your label mean?"

The customers then related the negative things they were focused on, how things are terrible and life is not fair.

But the owner kept talking about all the positive parts of life and his business:

- How rewarding it is to meet new customers all the time
- How it is a great privilege to serve the community
- How much he loves helping other farmers grow their crops

This attitude had a domino effect on the employees. His act of positivity and enthusiasm became infectious. His employees were empowered and learned a positive attitude from the farmer. Even when things were tough, and they were struggling, everyone focused on a positive outlook.

That's what you need in your career and your business. You need to be positive and empower your team to stay positive. You will build an empire.

Frontline Leader

About two hundred years ago, a rider passed a group of exhausted soldiers who were digging themselves into an important defensive position. The rider noticed that the soldiers' defensive leader was shouting and yelling at the men to dig deeper, faster. He threatened to whip anyone who did not complete his work on time.

Then the rider asked the defensive commander, "If this is so important, why are you not helping?"

The commander replied that he was in charge and the soldiers had to follow orders. Then he said to the rider, "If you feel so strongly about it, you should help the soldiers yourself."

The rider dismounted and worked in the trench with the soldiers until the job was finished. He then congratulated the soldiers for a job well done.

The rider approached the defense commander and said, "Next time your rank prevents you from supporting your men, you are to notify top command, and I will provide a more permanent solution."

This rider was General George Washington. Some of you may have heard of his extraordinary leadership ability.

The point is clear. If you want to empower others, you must be willing to get in the trenches with your employees. You must be willing to do the work of your team without compliant when they need you the most. You must be visible and supportive at all times. You must be at the frontline and leave a path for your followers to follow.

If you want your employees or staff to be enthusiastic, you must be enthusiastic. If you want your team to be positive, you must be a positive leader.

Monkey see; monkey do.

Empower and Let Go

Letting go is a phrase often used in reference to forgiving someone. It has a connotation of freedom or forgiveness. It frees you to do other things. It frees your mind so you can think about other things. It frees your mind so you can think about growing yourself or your empire.

Many successful companies and organizations today succeed because of empowering others, letting go of their authority, and sharing with others. No one wants to be micromanaged. Everyone loves to be independent as they go about their daily activities.

For you and your business to grow, you must empower and let go.

John Timpson is a successful business owner in Europe. He believes in sharing power with his employees. He provides a thorough training program and gives his employees access to up to five hundred Euros to solve customers' issues. This means he entrusts his employees with solving customers' issues and problems quickly and efficiently. His business grows exponentially.

Disneyworld is known for their guests' experience with cast members, ensuring every touch point is magical. Disney empowers their staff by a simple demonstration of genuine care: They listen to their staff. They make sure they thank their staff. They share positive customers' experience. Disney has built an empire just by empowering their staff and recognizing each and every one of them.

Google is a world-renowned innovative company. They nurture creativity and build an environment where creativity thrives in an inclusive work environment. The company has what are called *Google Cafes,* which encourage their staff to interact with people from other departments—they share ideas for both work and play. They also allow engineers to send 20 percent of their workweek on projects that interest them. This encourages them to explore their own ideas and bring new services and products to the company.

These are just a few examples of companies across the globe that nurture employees' empowerment.

Remember, for your business or organization to succeed you must:

- Empower and let go.
- Be the cheerleader in a nurturing positive environment.
- Be on the frontline with your team.
- Let go of some of your own power and authority.

CHAPTER FIVE

Freedom at Last!

HOW FREEDOM FEELS

According to the *Encyclopedia of Marxism,* freedom is defined as "the right and capacity of people to determine their own actions in a community which can provide for the full development of human potentiality." Freedom may be enjoyed by individuals but only in and through the community.

Did you notice in the definition that freedom is linked to your own action and the full development of human potential?

How do you determine your own action?

How do you develop full potential?

Answering these questions will help you to be free.

Determine Your Own Action

Almost everyone I have met in my life and personally interviewed has something in common. They all want to be free. So do I. We are all born with the inherent determination and right to be free. We all yearn to be free.

Quest for freedom has resulted in so many casualties in human history. However, freedom has also resulted in the success and advancement of human achievement. Freedom is an informed decision you must personally make.

Freedom is intentional.

To be truly free, you need to determine what true freedom really means to you. Everyone has their own definition of freedom. No matter how you define your own freedom, action must be taken to achieve and experience true freedom.

A popular quote on social media states, "The key to being where few people are is to start doing what few people do."

Only a few people can truly say that they are free and they love what they do. Those few people act; they act on what is needed to be truly free. They are intentional.

As you move forward, you need to:

1. Determine your *why*. Define what freedom means to you:

    ○ *Why do you want to be free?*

  - *How would freedom look a year from now, three years from now, five years from now?*

2. Determine your *what.* What do you need to do to achieve your true freedom? This answer defines your action steps.
3. Determine your *who.* Ask yourself these questions:
   - *Who do you need to become to achieve your freedom?*
   - *Who else can help you to achieve your freedom?*

Having discovered and identified these definitions in writing, act. This will not be a one-time action. You will need to review and amend these answers as you progress in your career; it's a lifelong endeavor. It doesn't come overnight.

Keep working on it. Persist until you succeed.

Now, let's discuss how you can develop your full potential, an important step in achieving your desired success.

Develop Your Full Potential

> *Lineage, personality, and environment may shape you, but they do not define your full potential.*
>
> ~ Mollie Marti

If lineage, personality, and environment do not determine your full potential, how then do you develop your full potential?

Let's first consider what *potential* means. According to the *Free Dictionary,* it simply means, "that which is possible, capable of being but not yet in existence; the inherent ability or capacity for growth, development, coming into being, or ability to be free." We are all born with this potential; it is neither nurture, in-born, nor nature, environmental. It is something we all need to develop.

If maximizing your full potential does not occur naturally, how then can this be developed?

There are three things you may want to consider as you develop your full potential. First, don't forget your youth. This might seem crazy.

Do you remember when you were young and vibrant and energetic?

Do you remember how you were full of excellent ideas?

When we are young, we have an open mind. We believe we can achieve and accomplish anything. Unfortunately, as we grow older we tend to hold back our thoughts because we fear ridicule. This fear inhibits our full potential.

Now, I want you to have that same youthful mind. Open your mind; allow the ideas to flow. Write them in a journal. Your ideas are like skeletons: you need to add meat to them and breathe into them so they come alive. Develop your ideas by writing action plans and steps to achieve them. Think about everything you are capable of doing and achieving. Begin working on it right away.

Second, do not be afraid to fail. Most people quit their dreams and ideas after one attempt. They simply give up on maximizing their full potential. You *will* make mistakes. Mistakes and failures are okay, provided you acknowledge them and learn from them.

Third, focus on your skills, your natural-born ability, your quest to make a difference in people's lives. Then, you will maximize your full potential. In the long run, you will find peace of mind that gives you freedom, freedom to do what you love to do, freedom to be unstoppable.

Your Freedom, Your Life

> *Go confidently in the direction of your dreams.*
> *Live the life you've imagined.*
>
> ~ Thoreau

To be truly free and live the life you imagine, you must continue to engage in what you love to do. You must follow your dream. Based on personal interviews, my impression is that 90 percent of people find themselves in jobs they hate. They find themselves doing work that does not give them inner peace, their true freedom.

So many of us have been taught the correct way to live. We feel obligated to live a certain life because of the expectations put on us by ourselves, our parents, and our society.

In 2006, I became a registered nurse. I felt I could live the life I desired. I believed I would be happy since my new career was a gateway for me to make more money and cherry-pick the job I wanted—wherever I wanted to work. In fact, my income did increase, and I was able to dictate how much money I would make.

A few years later, I felt enslaved. I feel like something was missing within me. I felt I wasn't making an impact on people's lives—my initial reason for becoming a nurse. I decided to quit my job and a few months later, I started a new company called Prestige Healthcare Resources. This company focuses on helping seniors to remain vibrant and age in the place they choose. We also help care givers live their life stress-free while caring for their loved ones.

After starting the company, I realized I wasn't stressed the way I used to be. Helping people in the community gave me joy and happiness. This new venture gave me the opportunity to travel and live the life I dreamed.

I began to realize what true freedom really means:

- Freedom from guilt
- Freedom to control my own life
- Freedom to control my own time
- Freedom to decide how much I wanted to make
- Freedom to empower others

Design the life you want to live today and experience true freedom.

LASTING FREEDOM THROUGH CONSISTENCY

Just as nobody *owns* success, nobody holds off success. People pay the price needed to create success. They pay every day. Failure to do this results in enslavement. The same is true with freedom. We must pay the price of reaching it. Not once, not twice, but at all times.

Here are three qualities you should develop to maintain your freedom.

The Act of Patience

Lack of patience is the number-one reason most people fail to experience success or true freedom. We live in a world where people want microwave success, results at the push of a button. Our society encourages this. We have a drive-through everything. We drive through to grab food, we drive through to wash cars, we drive through to buy liquor, we can even drive through to get married.

We should not waste time blaming our society for this quick-fix mentality. It's the century in which we found ourselves. While we cannot control everything that happens to us or our environment, we can at least control what we do about it.

You can develop a rare quality called *patience.* This quality will help you develop a realistic time frame for growth. It will help you to learn new skills and as you pursue the experiences you need to become a better you.

How long will it take?

It depends. It depends on what you want to achieve; it depends on your dreams. It depends on your resources. It might be frustrating to wait for that deal to come through. It might be frustrating waiting for that first check in the mail. It might be frustrating trying to find the right person to empower or motivate or employ. It might be frustrating striving to achieve your long-term goals.

If you persist and be patient, you will realize your goals are worth waiting for.

Take time to think about and appreciate what you gain along the way:

- Progress in becoming your best self
- Appreciation for the people you know
- New connections
- New circles of influence

As my dad often tells me whenever I get frustrated and impatient, "The patient dog eats the fattest bone."

If you are patient, you will build an empire. Harness this quality today and you are guaranteed success.

The Act of Focus

The *Pareto principle* states that 20 percent of the tasks you do are responsible for 80 percent of your success. This principle didn't make sense to me until a few years ago. When I founded my company, I was everywhere doing everything. I was very ambitious. I wanted to branch out everywhere. I informed our staff to accept any service request.

We then realized we were stretching ourselves too thin. We reviewed the services we had done in the past and focused on the ones we had done well. We decided to focus on these few services. We invested all our efforts, time, and energy into these areas. And the rest is history.

To experience true freedom, you must have laser focus. You must focus on one or two things you do very well and become *world-class* at them. This is what Apple did. When they put all their efforts into producing iPhones, they took over the world market of smartphones. They became world-class.

Another thing you need to learn is how to say *no*. Saying no frees you to focus on what is most important. For instance, if your goal is to be an author, your ability to say no to other things not related to being an author frees you to focus more on being an expert writer. Saying no means taking the time to focus on what makes you a world-class expert.

As you experience more success, you will also experience more distractions. You must control your time; you must control your attention.

As Darren Hardy, the founder of *Success* magazine says, "What controls your attention, controls your life."

You need to unplug electronic distractions and block out specific time daily for focusing.

These practices help me stay focused; try them for yourself:

- Block out specific time to focus mentally.
- Block out specific time for social media—thirty to sixty minutes daily.
- Create a distraction-free environment.
- Focus on single task at a time—avoid multitasking.
- Take regular breaks to re-energize.
- Monitor time spent on most common tasks.

In this century, we are bombarded with waves of information. Staying focused has become an essential commodity for all. If you consistently stay focused, you will attain and maintain true freedom and happiness no matter where you are in your quest for success.

The Power of Discipline

If you don't control yourself, you are controlled by your circumstances.

People often ask me what makes me successful. Well, the answer is in this ten-letter word: *discipline.* This is lesson one for all successful people. It is the basis for success; it is the secret to consistent freedom. It is, in fact, the basis for everything in life.

That's why people say, "Your level of success is determined by your level of discipline."

Ordinarily, the word discipline has a negative connotation. You may associate it with law enforcement, punishment, or restrictions. As a child, I remember all the rules I obeyed: when to wake up, when to eat, when to play. Many of us can relate to that. As an adult, we still must obey certain rules and regulations; we must follow policies and procedures at work. We must conform to a certain code of conduct in society.

However, as you mature you will notice that you change from *explicit* discipline to *implicit* discipline. You now have the choice to decide which discipline to follow and which to discard.

To be truly successful and maintain freedom, you must be *implicitly* disciplined. You must have routines in place. Develop daily habits for yourself, as if you were a child. Granted, these habits might change based on your circumstances and conditions, your goals and priorities. The point is, you must develop consistent, predictable habits and discipline yourself to stick with them.

John Maxwell says, "Small disciplines repeated with consistency every day lead to great achievements gained slowly over time."

You need consistent disciple to achieve your goals. You need consistent discipline to experience freedom.

Discipline *is* freedom.

Aristotle said, "through discipline comes freedom." Discipline yourself today and experience lasting freedom.

LIVE YOUR LEGACY

> *Only by giving are you able to receive more than you already have.*
>
> ~ Jim Rohn

You've reached your goals, achieved all the success you dreamed, maximized your potentials. You have built and grown your empire. And now, you feel something is missing. You are still not happy.

What is the missing piece?

Consider this quote from the Bible, written about two thousand years ago: "There is more happiness in giving than there is in receiving" (Acts 20:35, paraphrased).

Could this be the missing link for true happiness?

Definitely.

Author Albert Pine said, "What we do for ourselves dies with us. What we do for others and the world remains and is immortal."

If you want to leave a legacy, if you want to make a dent in the universe, give back.

The Law of Tithe

As a child, we had a little box in our classroom. My teacher told us to put in whatever was left of our lunch allowance. He used the money to buy hot food for the homeless. Later, I realized the lesson my teacher at the time was instilling in us—pay your tithe.

Most religious organizations have similar concepts of giving back. In ancient times, one nation, Israel, was mandated to give from their surplus to the needy and the poor among them. The nation was promised blessing and abundance. While there are no laws or rules mandating giving back to the community, this principle still applies today.

Most successful people pay their tithe in the form of a foundation or a cause they believe in.

Here are a few examples of successful people who give back to their communities:

1. Mark Zuckerberg, the founder of Facebook, donated $1 billion to the Silicon Valley Community Foundation via company stock in 2013.[1]

2. Charles Johnson, head of Franklin Resources, donated $250 million in 2013 to Yale University.[2]

3. Paul Allen donated $206 million largely to his own foundation, the Paul G. Allen Foundation, but also notably to the EMP (Experience Music Project) Museum in Seattle.[3]

4. Mark Cuba, owner of Dallas Mavericks, supports charitable activities in the Dallas area and throughout the United States.[4]

The list goes on and on. Let's be clear. You do not have to be a millionaire to give back to the community. What really counts is the motive behind your giving. Giving gives you a sense of happiness and success that money cannot buy.

---

1 businessinsider.com/biggest-philanthropists-2013-2014-2/#-frank-mccourt-1

2 Ibid.

3 Ibid.

4 forbes.com/sites/drewhendricks/2014/06/02/top-15-entrepreneurs-who-give-back-to-the-community/#238800165a4f

Reasons to Live

What is the purpose of life?

What is the reason to live?

I often find myself struggling to find answers to these questions. A few years ago, I woke up in the middle of the night. I was reminiscing about my life, about people I have known, about successful people I have encountered. I felt devastated and dejected.

A few hours prior to that moment, I came home from work. I was working as an on-call nurse for a hospice company. I had pronounced the death of five of our patients within two hours. As I walked into their multimillion-dollar homes, I knew they were wealthy and successful. But inevitably, they did not escape the sting of death. All the riches and success and money and influences did not add a minute to their lives.

I struggled with this feeling for weeks until I came to terms with myself. I finally realized that the reason to live this life is personal to everyone. My reason to live is not to accumulate wealth and riches and glory. My reason to live is to have an impact on everyone I encounter daily. My reason to live is to help people to live a fulfilled life. My reason to live is to help our aging population live a comfortable life, stress and worry free.

Take the time to answer these questions:

- What's your reason to live?
- What's your purpose?
- Are you here to accumulate wealth?
- Are you here to help others – to give back to the community?

Find your reason to live. Write it down and live with it.

Sense of Fulfillment

Fulfillment is a feeling of satisfaction that comes when you complete a task, when you reach your goals. Unfortunately, as humans we are created with a quest to want more, do more, and achieve more.

Fifteen years ago, prior to migrating to the United States, I went through a lot of suffering and torture. I escaped rebel attacks and death on numerous occasions. I could not attend college during the ten years after I graduated from high school due to the civil war in Liberia. I always dreamt of coming to America. I thought coming to the United States would give me all I wanted in life. Fortunately, I eventually found myself in one of the greatest countries in the world, the United States of America.

Then I thought: *If only I could go to college, I will be fulfilled.*

I went to college and graduated as a nurse.

Then I thought: *If only I could start my own business, I will be fulfilled.*

I started my own business.

Then I thought: *If only I could get the business to make millions, I will be fulfilled.*

My business made millions.

As long as you exist, you will always be pulled by:

- Things to do
- Goals to achieve
- Obligations to meet

When will you draw the line of achieving true fulfillment and satisfaction?

How will you know when you experience a sense of fulfillment?

A sense of fulfillment is defined differently by everyone. I believe that to experience true satisfaction and a sense of fulfillment, you need to celebrate and experience every accomplishment you make, no matter how small it is. This celebration will act as a catalyst to help you achieve your bigger goals—your big, hairy, audacious goals.

I remember receiving our first check for our company. I believe it was a little over two hundred dollars. We celebrated, we enlarged a photocopy of the check, and we framed it. We hung it on the wall. We had sense of fulfillment for that accomplishment.

Celebrate success on your journey to the city of true happiness and freedom—the place where you have total control of your time, total control of your life, and total control of everything that happens to you. Don't leave it to chance. Design the type of freedom you desire and live your desired life.

Conclusion

If you have followed my instructions to this point, you are bound to make a difference in people's lives!

No matter where you are in your journey to success, you need to continue to refine your *why*. You need to identify if you are truly making the impact you are meant to make in people's lives. Your purpose is not to be successful and keep that success to yourself. True happiness and satisfaction will come when you influence the community.

Success is never earned. It is borrowed. Be willing to pay what it takes every day of your journey. Remember, your success is someone else's miracle.

As you move forward:

- Continue to empower the generation to come.
- Continue to empower your community.
- Continue to be consistent in your quest for sustainable success.
- Continue to impact people's lives.
- Continue to make a difference.

You are sure to succeed.

Take a moment to make this list, writing three items for each:

1. Reasons you want to make a difference in people's lives
2. Self-limiting beliefs or setbacks
3. Ideas or problems you are willing to solve
4. People you can empower
5. What you want to be remembered for

Whether you are thinking of starting your own business or a new start-up as solopreneur or entrepreneur, one thing that you need is to understand how to leverage yourself. Understanding this has helped me tremendously in my career and my business. My goal is to assist you in finding and identifying areas in your life and business where you can outsource, so you can focus more on working on your *why*.

What's easy to do is also easy not to do.

Knowing what to do and bringing it to reality are two different things. We would like to be your accountability partner and join you on the journey to your success.

Next Steps

Visit our websites, YourFreedomYourLife.com & FreedomAtLastBook.com where you may download lists and resources. These resources will help you leverage your time, efforts, and resources.

About the Author

John Saye Smith is the founder of Prestige Healthcare Resources (PHR) DBA Personnel Results, an in-home care, case management, and staffing agency focusing on enhancing the lifestyles of nurses and other professionals.

He graduated with an associate's degree in nursing at Prince Georges' Community College and then received a bachelor's degree in nursing at University of Maryland, Baltimore. He is currently pursuing his MBA degree.

Mr. Smith has been invited to speaking engagements on numerous occasions to share his stories with the world and to help individuals and companies learn the secrets of *How to Use Rejections as YOUR Weapon for Success*. He has been an inspirational icon for new companies, new employees, students, and people on the corporate ladder.

An immigrant to the United States who survived a civil war in Liberia, he is determined to be successful, to make a difference, and to be the best in what he does. His persistence has earned him the nickname, "The No Excuse Guy."

Mr. Smith enjoys spending time with his family, working out, and playing tennis, ping-pong, and volleyball.

www.ingramcontent.com/pod-product-compliance
Lightning Source LLC
Chambersburg PA
CBHW052119090426
42741CB00009B/1871

9781945446351